Train Your Brain

A model to help understand and regulate emotions

Tatterdemalion Blue

Published by Tatterdemalion Blue in 2025

A CIP catalogue record for this book is available
from the British Library

Cover design and layout by barbacreative.com

ISBN 978-1-915123-10-7

Tatterdemalion Blue
74 Maxwell Place
Stirling FK8 1JU

www.tatterdemalionblue.com

Train Your Brain

A model to help understand
and regulate emotions

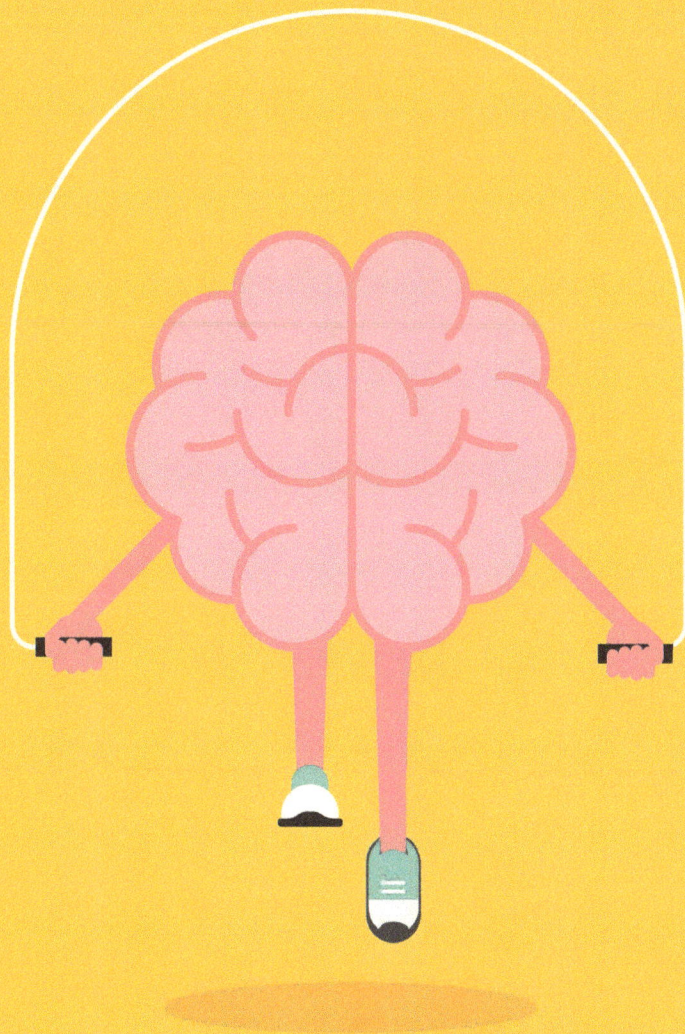

Dr Ståle Rygh and Dr Adam Morgan

Clinical Psychologists at Real Life Psychology CIC

Contents

Introduction

Life at times can feel like an obstacle course, leaving us with painful and unbearable emotions. This is especially true when we experience difficult and traumatic events whilst we are growing up or as an adult. Whilst pain and suffering are often unavoidable in such circumstances, how we manage our reactions to these difficulties can make a significant difference to the extent of our suffering. In the face of these problems, we might tell ourselves to 'pull ourselves together' and 'get on with it', or we may see our difficulties as a sign of weakness, launching into self-attack. These responses may be common in our society, but they are unlikely to help us learn and recover from setbacks, and may even deepen or prolong our suffering.

In Train your Brain we introduce a different approach to responding to difficult emotions. Turning towards our emotions with curiosity gives us insight into our suffering, which can help us respond to these obstacles more skilfully. An important and hopeful message from neuro sciences is that our brain remains plastic throughout our lifetime. So, no matter how bruised, scarred or broken we might feel from our path through life, or whatever age we are, our brain is able to recover and learn new ways to respond to the difficulties we face. We hope that the ideas in this book can help you better understand yourself and how your brain works, and together with the exercises, assist you in navigating life for both joy and success.

Understanding your Self

Focus of the Train Your Brain Course

The aim of Train Your Brain is twofold: firstly, to help you better understand your thoughts and feelings, and secondly, to strengthen your ability to manage these more skilfully.

We will look at how the brain generates thoughts, feelings and physical sensations, pleasant and unpleasant. We will then explore the role of attention, breathing, imagery, the body, and the relationship we have with ourselves and people around us in fostering good mental health. Train Your Brain is designed as a guided self-help course where we will introduce tried and tested practices to bring some perspective and balance to our thinking and dampen overwhelming emotions. These practices form part of an emotion-regulation toolkit that can help us respond skilfully to the various challenges life throws at us.

Like anything in life we want to become better at, we need regular practice. An emerging observation from brain science is 'neuroplasticity', meaning that the brain is malleable throughout our life. So, just like we need to do regular weightlifting if we want our muscles to grow and become stronger, for our brain to develop and become more functional, we need to give it a regular workout.

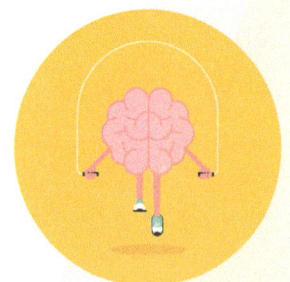

Emotional Intelligence

Whereas conventional intelligence is thought to be relatively fixed throughout our lifetime, emotional intelligence (the capacity to understand and manage our emotions effectively) can be developed and improved significantly over time. Emotional intelligence helps us to navigate life skilfully.

Self-regulation is seen as a central component of emotional intelligence; it helps us manage impulses, engage or disengage attention, and navigate between deliberate or automatic responses. This enables us to keep in control of challenging thoughts and feelings, stay focused on what matters to us, and maintain constructive relationships with people in our life.

Emotions can be hard to understand and harder still to manage. However, without the ability to understand and manage our emotions, our internal and social lives can become pretty chaotic. Sometimes we can be unaware or neglectful of our emotions, or we may try to numb them by any means possible (alcohol, drugs, food, gambling, sex etc). However, although this may offer temporary respite from our difficult emotions, it tends to deepen our distress in the long run.

Emotions are akin to waves in the sea, we may not be able to stop them, but we can learn to ride them skilfully and this is the very essence of emotional intelligence.

The Shaping of our Brain

The brain is an extraordinary organ capable of exceptional feats. However, just like a seed needs nutritious soil, sufficient water and sunlight in order to germinate into a healthy plant, human beings need an environment that is physically safe and emotionally supportive in order for our brains to develop fully. Genetics certainly play an important role in how our brains are shaped; however, the quality of our environment plays an equally (and some would say larger) part in how we turn out. The study of the interplay between our genes and environment is called epigenetics. Epigenetic studies show that positive environmental factors (such as supportive relationships) actually 'turn on' good genes, so by making changes to our social environment, we can make changes to how our brain operates.

Whilst it is fair to say that there is much we do not know about the brain and its workings, many theories talk about there being three main parts of the brain that develop from gestation through to the finished product in our early 20s.

Brain Stem: the instinctive brain
It receives input from the feeling and reasoning brain and responds appropriately, either firing up or calming down.

Limbic: the feeling brain
The limbic system is like a radar; we register what is going on in the external and internal world and this generates lots of sensory information like thoughts, feelings, images, and bodily sensations (e.g., I see something dangerous and I feel fear and an impulse to run away).

Cortex: the reasoning brain
This is the conscious part of our brain. It analyses the raw data of the limbic system and makes decisions about whether and how we act on emotions and impulses. This cortex enables us to reflect, plan, organize, problem-solve and speak.

Cortex

Limbic

Brain Stem

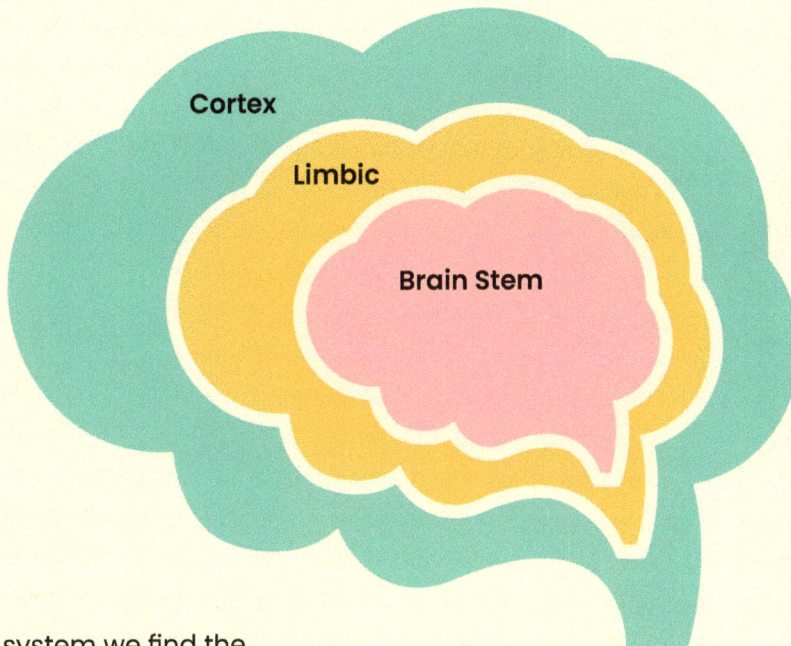

Within the limbic system we find the Amygdala, which is like a threat detector. To give you an idea of how this works, consider the following example; You are going for a woodland walk and all of a sudden you spot an s-shaped object ahead of you on the path. As soon as your Amygdala (threat detector) spots this potential threat, it sounds the alarm, which immediately activates the fight, flight, freeze response, resulting in you freezing on the spot or pulling away. This threat response is immediate and automatic and something you have no or very limited control over. Our brain operates on the 'better safe than sorry' principle; it's a more successful survival strategy to assume that what you are facing is a threat and respond accordingly, than assuming the opposite and only discovering too late that you are facing a threat you can't protect yourself from.

Having taken action and jumped away from the s-shaped object, the cortex now comes into play. A key role of the cortex is to discern between real threats and false alarms. In this instance the cortex works like a zoom. Getting a close-up view of this potential threat, it might then notice that the s-shaped object is not a snake but in fact just a twig.

The cortex then tells the Amygdala/Limbic system that it's a false alarm, the fight, flight and freeze mode gets turned off, and it is safe to proceed.

However, there are times when the communication between the cortex and Amygdala/Limbic system breaks down. If a person has suffered a lot of trauma then the threat system is used a lot and can become easily triggered. The consequence is that it will often raise false alarms and the person can get stuck in a state of threat. In effect, the person sees snakes everywhere!

The same brain systems operate when we are faced with social and interpersonal threats. If we are criticised by someone who matters to us, such as a manager or a partner, the Amygdala/Limbic system can fire up in exactly the same was as when we face a physical threat. The consequence of this is we lose access to our reasoning brain and are driven by our emotions and threat response, perhaps saying or doing things we will later regret.

Fight, Flight, Freeze and Fawn

When we feel threatened, an automatic physiological response within us, often called 'fight, flight, freeze or fawn', is activated. This response has evolved as it increases our chances of survival when in danger.

The fight, flight, freeze or fawn response is automatic and involves the activation of our sympathetic nervous system.

It diverts blood and oxygen to our large muscle groups, turns off our thinking mind (our cortex) and releases various stress hormones into our blood. The effect of all this is that our heart beats faster, our breathing speeds up, our pupils dilate and we are ready to fight or run (or sometimes just freeze on the spot). As well as this, all our attention will focus on the threat we have spotted and we won't take in other information.

'Fawning', also called please and appease, is a trauma response where a person behaves in a way to appease an aggressor in order to avoid conflict and harm and ensure safety.

It is important to stress that when in fight, flight, freeze or fawn mode, it limits conscious control of our behaviours. Sometimes people can look back at a traumatic situation and blame themselves, for not calling out for help (freezing), running away from an injured person (fleeing) or for not stopping unwanted sexual advances (fawning).

Understanding what is happening when this is triggered can help us to feel less panicked about it and do things to settle us down again. It is not a sign that we are crazy or out of control, but an automatic physiological reaction to believing we are in danger.

Emotional Emergency Plan

Whilst the practices in this toolkit will help in the long term, here are some short-term things you can try in an 'emotional emergency'.

It can help to write these ideas down on a flash card, or on your phone and carry them with you.

Posture – try to open up your posture. Go for a slow walk and try naming some of the things you can see around you.

Breathing – try to slow and deepen your breathing. This is always a useful practice in everyday life.

Affirmation – remind yourself, this moment will pass, these emotions are not permanent.

Growing Up

As young children, we haven't as yet developed much of a cortex, therefore our ability to regulate feelings and impulses is very limited.

As children we need balanced caregivers around us to help us manage our feelings. If we have caregivers who are reliably present and attuned to the difficulties we bring to them as children, their presence and soothing words or touch, quickly and effectively help us to feel better (by dampening down our limbic system). This leaves us feeling safe and calm and we can return to focus fully on whatever is important to us. In effect children can 'borrow' the emotional intelligence (or cortex) of their caregivers to help them manage their feelings when things are difficult.

We call this process **co-regulation**; the child brings their distress to the adult, who in turn offers comfort. If this co-regulation happens consistently over time, the child is likely to grow up to be an adult who can self-regulate in times of difficulties. In essence the input we get from our caregivers stimulates our cortex, and like a muscle, it gets stronger and more effective.

If on the other hand, we don't have a caregiver to turn to when we are distressed, or the caregiver is either inattentive, dismissive or abusive, our distress remains or deepens. Inattentive or dismissive caregivers often have their own troubles and difficulties which impact on their ability to manage their own emotions. These caregivers often struggle to effectively manage their children's distress.

There is no such thing as perfect parenting and moments of inattentiveness or frustration are very unlikely to cause significant harm. What children need is 'good enough' parenting so that they feel safe and loved.

Sadly, many children grow up in environments that are neglectful and abusive. For the child this is when tolerable, fleeting stress can become toxic, permanent stress. In this way, we can struggle to learn effective ways to self-regulate as adults. We may develop a belief that negative emotions can't be tolerated or changed and then seek external ways to self soothe, such as using substances.

If we grew up in an environment where we felt unsettled or unsafe, our limbic system (that perceives and responds to threats) can get over-sensitive, contributing to overwhelming feelings, such as anger, fear, jealousy, shame etc., and trigger strong urges and cravings. In combination with a cortex that struggles to effectively dampen these feelings, the consequence can be impulsive and self-defeating thoughts, feelings and actions.

It is important to notice that whilst we are clearly not responsible for the environment that shaped our brain, it is possible to try and understand and manage the difficulties that these experiences have led to. We can then learn to act in ways that minimise harm to ourselves and the people around us.

For example, if we are the victim of an unprovoked act of vandalism, such as our car being smashed up, that's clearly not our fault, however, it is possible for us to repair the car so it's roadworthy and in good shape. Now whilst this isn't exactly 'fair' it does leave us with a working car.

Our brain has evolved different capacities that can sometimes have unwanted consequences.

The part of our brain that protects us from danger (limbic system/threat response), is also the part of the brain that generates anxiety and makes it hard to relax and enjoy ourselves.

And whilst our cortex allows us to plan for the future and reflect on events in the past, which is key to organizing our lives, we can get stuck ruminating about negative past events or worrying about endless disasters in the future, which can make us overwhelmed and unhappy.

Emotional intelligence (the ability to regulate our emotions and stay within our window of tolerance) can be improved by having some knowledge of the workings of the brain and using this knowledge to keep our minds balanced.

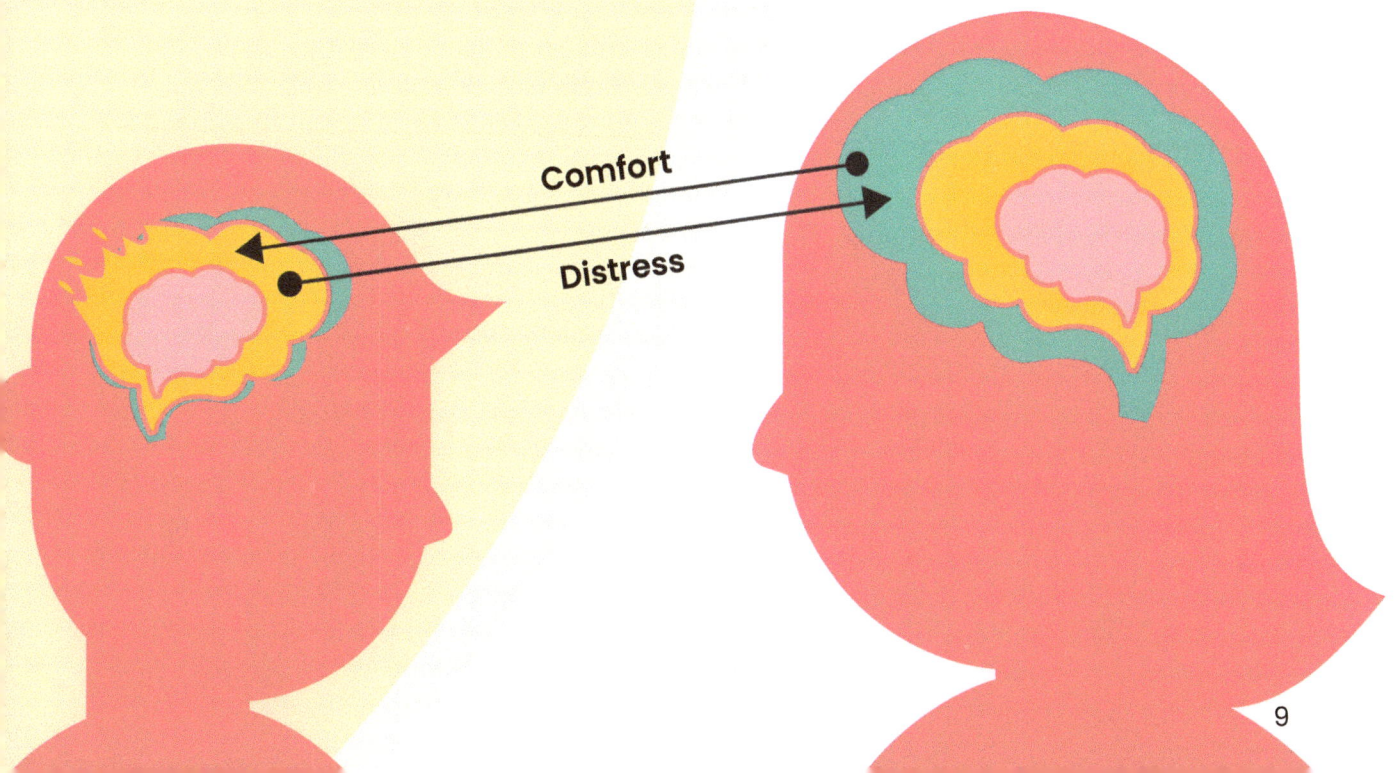

Comfort

Distress

Window of Tolerance

Window of tolerance refers to the optimal zone of arousal for a person to function in everyday life. When we are within our window of tolerance (calm arousal), we have full access to our cortex, the part of our brain that enables us to think about challenges in a balanced way, make sensible decisions and communicate effectively. When we experience hurt, anxiety, pain and anger, this may bring us close to the edges of our window of tolerance. However, these emotions tend to naturally subside over time, or we may use calming strategies that bring the distress down to a tolerable level.

Similarly, we may feel exhausted, low, or shut down, but we may naturally restore our equilibrium once we have rested and recharged, or we may engage in activities or practices that lift our mood and energy.

If a person has experienced significant adverse life events, such as trauma, they may have a smaller window of tolerance, so that even seemingly minor stressors can lead to states of hyperarousal (fight/flight) or hypoarousal (freeze).

Some people get stuck in high levels of Activation (inability to stay calm - fight/flight) or Deactivation (shutting down - freeze) involuntarily when confronted with stress.

In a hyperarousal state, we are more likely to overestimate the dangers of a situation and underestimate our ability to cope, sometimes resulting in avoidant or impulsive behaviours that can make the situation worse.

In a hypoarousal state, we may feel unable to think, make decisions or act all together, leaving us feeling out of control and helpless.

A key aim of Train Your Brain is to increase our window of tolerance so that we can deal with challenges more proactively and skilfully.

We can achieve this by being curious about our emotions, rather than judging or suppressing them. This can help us better understand, accept, tolerate, express and regulate emotions.

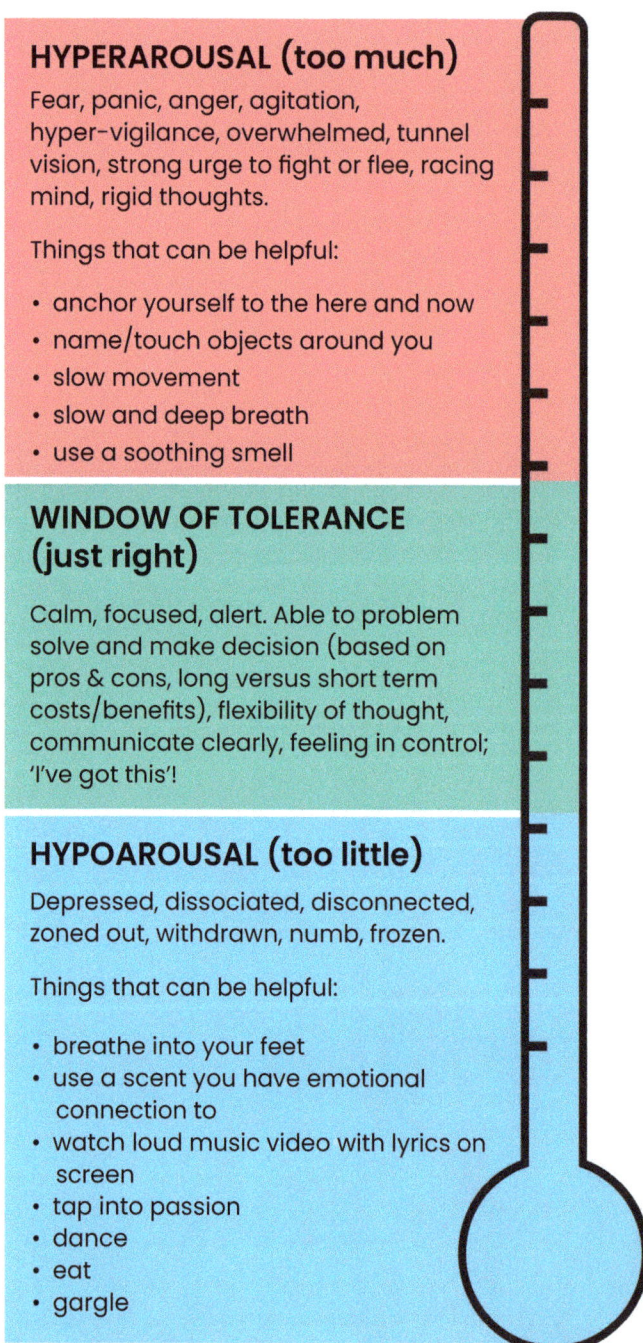

HYPERAROUSAL (too much)

Fear, panic, anger, agitation, hyper-vigilance, overwhelmed, tunnel vision, strong urge to fight or flee, racing mind, rigid thoughts.

Things that can be helpful:

- anchor yourself to the here and now
- name/touch objects around you
- slow movement
- slow and deep breath
- use a soothing smell

WINDOW OF TOLERANCE (just right)

Calm, focused, alert. Able to problem solve and make decision (based on pros & cons, long versus short term costs/benefits), flexibility of thought, communicate clearly, feeling in control; 'I've got this'!

HYPOAROUSAL (too little)

Depressed, dissociated, disconnected, zoned out, withdrawn, numb, frozen.

Things that can be helpful:

- breathe into your feet
- use a scent you have emotional connection to
- watch loud music video with lyrics on screen
- tap into passion
- dance
- eat
- gargle

Adverse Childhood Events

The significant and long lasting impact of adversity in our early life has been highlighted by a collection of studies in the US in the 1990s named the ACE studies. ACE stands for adverse childhood event, and includes incidences of emotional, physical or sexual abuse amongst other traumatic events. The findings showed a clear trend that the more ACEs a person has experienced in their childhood, the more health and social problems they will experience through their lifetime (the table below clearly shows this trend).

In essence, early adversity can mean our threat system gets stuck on high alert, leaving us feeling unsafe and on edge. This can lead to problems with our mental health and the use of drugs and alcohol to cope with things. Over time, this puts a huge toll on our mind and body, making us less resilient to stress and illness, and a difficulty trusting and bonding with others. The good news is that we now know that our brain remains adaptable throughout our lifespan and we can learn to feel safe and live a fulfilling life even after a difficult start.

Significant Experiences		
Given 100 American Adults		
33 No ACEs	51 1-3 ACEs	16 4-8 ACEs
With 0 ACEs	With 3 ACEs	With 7+ ACEs
1 in 16 smokes	1 in 9 smokes	1 in 6 smokes
1 in 69 is alcoholic	1 in 9 is alcoholic	1 in 6 is alcoholic
1 in 480 uses IV drugs	1 in 43 uses IV drugs	1 in 30 uses IV drugs
1 in 14 has heart disease	1 in 7 has heart disease	1 in 6 has heart disease
1 in 96 attempts suicide	1 in 10 attempts suicide	1 in 5 attempts suicide

Making sense of it all – what psychologists call 'formulation'

When trying to help someone with their struggles psychologists often work on creating what they call a 'formulation'. This is a way of making sense of how we end up where we are today: thinking, feeling and behaving the way we do.

Developing a formulation involves gathering important information about different parts of our life and linking this information together. This process is a bit like putting together pieces of a jigsaw and what we end up with is a coherent story, or a road map that can help us understand the path we have travelled on and also identify alternative, better paths going forward.

Have you ever found yourself turning down something you really want, such as an invitation to a social event or a job opportunity, ending a relationship that is going well, or getting drunk the night before an important exam?

At times we can act in ways that on the surface seem nonsensical and self-defeating. However, our behaviours and actions always have a function, no matter how illogical they may appear. Behaviours we deem to be unacceptable can bring strong feelings of shame, which can make us push these behaviours out of our mind. This means we are unlikely to understand and learn from past unhelpful behaviours and more likely to repeat our mistakes in the future.

Many people who have sought help for their mental health difficulties have been faced with the question 'what is wrong with you?'. The response to this might have resulted in a mental health diagnosis, may be Post Traumatic Stress Disorder, Recurrent Depressive Disorder, Emotionally Unstable Personality Disorder etc.

Although there can certainly be benefits to a diagnosis, it doesn't help us understand why we experience certain thoughts, feelings or behaviours. Shifting the focus to 'what has happened to me?' is likely to lead to a deeper, more nuanced understanding of our current difficulties.

By linking together significant experiences in our life with how they made us feel and what we have done to cope, we can help create a more compassionate understanding of why we think, feel and behave as we do.

There are many ways to go about making sense of our life experiences and how we have coped with them. One simple model that is relatively easy to follow is that used by the compassion-focused therapies developed by Paul Gilbert.

The first part of the process looks at significant experiences:

We know that early experiences and relationships that make us feel safe and cared about are key to good physical and emotional health throughout our life. However, when trying to understand the problems that we face in life it can be helpful to reflect on experiences that left us feeling unsafe or not cared about.

This could be incidences of physical, sexual or emotional abuse, or physical or emotional neglect (in effect Adverse Childhood Events, ACEs). It is the experiences that triggered our fight, flight, freeze or fawn response that can help us to understand the struggles that we face as adults.

The second part of the formulation is looking at the fears (beliefs) we have developed as a result of these significant negative experiences:

These fears might relate to us, for example that we are unsafe or vulnerable, that we have no worth or value. We might have fears about other people; we can't trust others or fear that others don't care or might take advantage of us. Lastly, we may have formed fears that the world is unsafe, unpredictable and hostile. In fact, when we formed these beliefs, these fears may well have just been the facts of our life at the time.

The third part of the formulation relates to safety strategies we may have developed:

These safety strategies are typically formed in response to real threats we have faced and their function is to protect us against future harm.

For example, if we have repeatedly been let down by a parent in times of need, we might have formed a fear that people don't care about us and can't be relied on. These fears may in turn give rise to a safety strategy of keeping people at arm's length and being self-reliant at all times.

The fourth section of the formulation looks at unintended consequences:

Safety strategies can be thought of as solutions we generate to problems we face. However, sometimes our solutions can make our problems bigger, not smaller.

If our solution to social anxiety is to avoid any social activities, we are likely to find that our confidence to manage social situations will diminish over time and our social anxiety is likely worsen. Moreover, if we avoid most interactions with people, we may become increasingly isolated, and we are likely to feel lonely and depressed.

Once we have linked all the four sections of the formulation together, we can start to see how some of our present day feelings, thoughts, beliefs and behaviour make complete sense when understood as reasonable responses to the challenges we have faced in life.

This in itself is often very helpful in managing how we feel about ourselves and may well help us to feel less shameful or guilty about how we have coped.

As well as this we can also reflect upon things. Are our fears or belief systems up to date? Are my safety strategies still needed or helpful?

If, as a child, we live in an unsafe environment and are harmed by our caregivers, or not protected from harm, then fears of being vulnerable and not being able to trust others reflect the reality of our situation. A safety strategy of being constantly on guard (hypervigilance) and keeping people at arm's length may help us survive.

However, if we fast-forward a decade or two and we are now an adult and being surrounded by people we can trust, these belief systems and safety strategies may no longer be necessary or helpful. In fact, they may stop us from connecting with people and living life fully, leaving us feeling depressed.

By practising different strategies, such as sharing or connecting more with people, putting ourselves forward for opportunities coming our way, we might have experiences that can help us see wourselves in a more positive light and our outlook might start to recalibrate in a more positive way.

Formulation

Example

Significant Experiences	Fears (or beliefs about self, others, the world)	Safety Strategies	Unintended Consequences
One parent being depressed, absent, withdrawn and unresponsive	I'm worthless, my needs and wants are unimportant	Ignore own needs, self-sacrifice	Feeling exploited, uncared for; growing feelings of resentment and low self-worth
An angry parent, unpredictable mood, quick to snap, particularly when drunk	I'm vulnerable, the world is unsafe	Being on guard, keeping others at arms' length	Feeling on edge, unable to relax or feeling uncomfortable in the company of others, social isolation
A critical teacher, being shouted at when making mistakes, being called 'stupid'	I'm not good enough, mistakes are unacceptable	Perfectionism, unrelenting standards	Exhaustion, anxiety about being found out, burnout

Now you have a go!

Significant Experiences	Fears (or beliefs about self, others, the world)	Safety Strategies	Unintended Consequences

Summary

As we have seen, our early social environment shapes our mind in important ways. If our immediate environment was characterised by danger, chaos and limited protection, comfort or guidance from adults, our mind might get stuck in 'threat mode' and the world we live in and people in it might seem unsafe and hostile.

We also looked at formulation which can be a good way to make sense of how our past experiences have shaped our thoughts, feelings and behaviours.

The good news is that our brain remains 'plastic' throughout our lives. This means it is capable of change and we can learn how to regulate our emotions and sooth the difficult feelings we are struggling with. In what follows we will go through a range of exercises you can try that will give your brain and mind a 'work out' and help it develop some of the emotion regulation skills that help life feel manageable.

We have split these emotion regulation skills into three parts.

First, we will focus on things that help us to dampen down our stress levels.

Second, we move more towards looking at ways we can re-assess the difficulties we are facing to make them more manageable and importantly reduce feelings of self-blame and guilt.

Finally, we will look at strengths and the things that you already do well but might not spend much time thinking about, or even realise are strengths that you have.

In the sections that follow it is fine to make use of those techniques that fit for you and to skip over any that don't. We are all different and things that make perfect sense to one person and work well for them, won't necessarily be helpful to someone else.

Train Your Brain Exercises

Soothing your Self

Re-focus

Focus on Strengths

Realistic Expectations

Like any learning process, learning new ideas and skills can be difficult. We may struggle with attention, concentration, memory, energy or motivation. It can be tempting when learning something new to be a little impatient, perhaps expecting too much too soon and set the bar too high.

We then strive towards our target, but fall short and conclude we have failed. This can quickly lead to feelings of hopelessness and frustration, and rather than spurring us on to do better next time, we are more likely to become demotivated and give up.

On a neurological level, if we aren't reaching the standards set by others or ourself, we often get a release of the stress hormone cortisol, and an excessive amount of this certainly doesn't help us learn!

If on the other hand, we set the bar within reach and achieve what we set out to achieve, we get a release of Dopamine, which is the very chemical that helps us feel motivated and energised.

The concept of dynamic goal setting can be useful to ensure our goals are helpful

If your goal is to be physically active and get into running, there will be various obstacles you will come up against in keeping up your exercise, that may vary from day to day. For example, cold, wet windy weather, how much you have slept, the presence of aches and pains etc.

On a day when there are few obstacles, it may be realistic to set yourself a goal of running a few miles and you get the neurochemical boost of this as well as the Dopamine release for reaching your goals.

If the next day, you haven't slept well and feel more achy, maybe a more realistic goal would be a 1 mile fast walk, and even if the cardiovascular boost might be less than a longer run, you get a Dopamine boost and prevent adding more stress-hormones by falling short of your goal.

Breathing

We know that breathing helps regulate our autonomic nervous system. We can think of deep breathing serving a similar function to the clutch in a car - it allows us to change to the most suitable mode for the challenge we are facing; a low gear for a hill start, and a high gear for driving on the motorway. Similarly, fast and shallow breathing sends oxygen to our muscles and activates the fight & flight mode, getting us ready for a quick get away or a defence/attack. This is exactly what is needed if we are faced with an imminent physical threat. However, this mode is unlikely to be helpful if we are faced with threats or challenges of a social nature, such as rejections, criticism, etc. Slow and deep breathing on the other hand, activates the parasympathetic nervous system, which helps us relax and recover after periods of activity and stress. Slow and deep breathing also helps redirect blow flow to the cortex, (or 'thinking brain') so that we can think, problem solve, communicate and interact effectively.

This is clearly beneficial if we are faced with an immediate physical threat we need to get away from. However, for most of us the kind of threats that activates this fight, flight, freeze response is of a psycho-social nature (a criticism, or a rejection, real or imagined), and in these instances we need to be able to think in order to generate a helpful answer/response, rather than running away. Therefore, we need to make sure that our cortex, or thinking brain, is fully online, and available to us.

Here is an exercise that helps you develop a soothing rhythm of breathing:

One of the most effective ways of doing this is to slow and deepen our breathing. Sit comfortably and take slow deep breaths. To ensure your breaths are deep you should be able to see your stomach rising and falling as you breath.

Now start to create a gap between each of your breaths. Breathe in slowly and hold your breath for a short time, then breathe out and again hold your breath for a short time. In this way you can create four equal parts to your breathing. Breathing in (1), waiting (2), breathing out (3) and again waiting (4) before breathing in again etc.

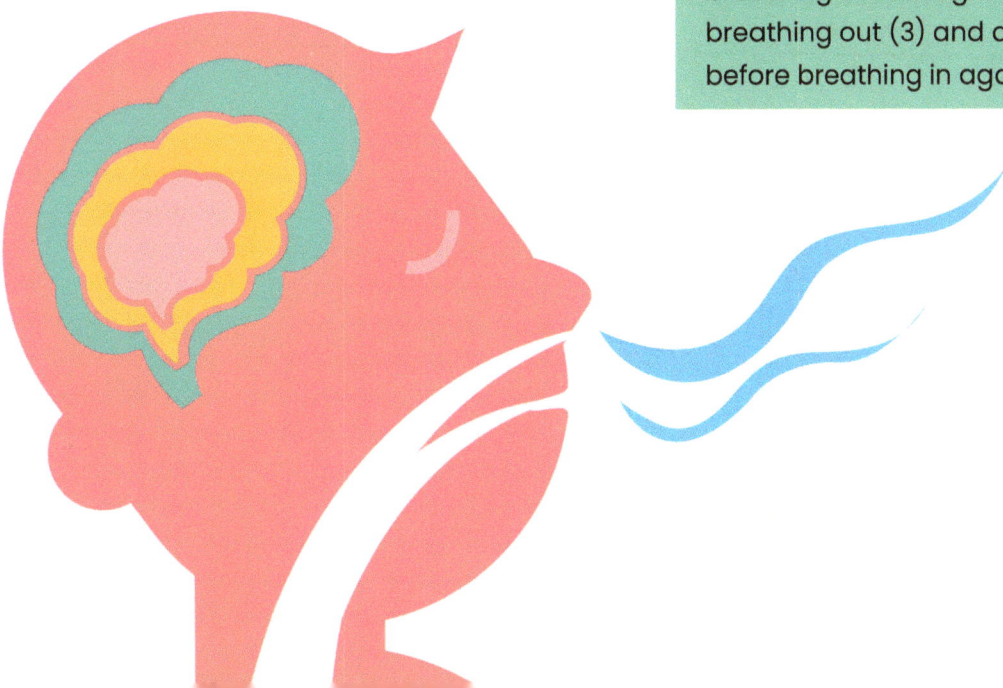

Meditation

Meditation has been around for thousands of years and can be a good way to start to build a healthy 'inside' life. Whilst our lives can be complicated and difficult it is important to remember to focus on the positive things that it is possible for us to be and feel.

Sit comfortably with your hands palm up on your lap. Breathe deeply and slowly as in the breathing exercise. Spend a couple of minutes getting used to this slow breathing.

Now take your right hand and place it on the centre of your stomach. Say to yourself "I am peace". See if you can feel the silence and peace of this moment. Spend a few moments with the sensation of peace within you.

Now move your hand to the centre of your chest. Say to yourself "I am love", "I love and respect myself". As you breathe see if you can feel this love within you. Spend a few moments with the sensation of love within you.

Now place your right hand on the top of your head, palm down. Say to yourself "I am free". Put your hand back on your lap and spend a few moments concentrating on this sense of freedom within you.

Now see if you can concentrate on the area above your head (above your mind) without thinking. When you are ready you can open your eyes.

Try to take these feelings with you into your day.

Body

You may have noticed that your mood and body posture are somehow connected.

When you feel confident and energetic, you may a have a more upright, open body posture, head up high and comfortably able to make eye contact.

However, if your mood is low, and you feel vulnerable, ashamed or anxious, you may have noticed that your body seems to shrink and close off, with your head turning down and avoiding eye contact. Some studies have shown that this 'low power pose' can increase cortisol and reduce testosterone.

This is important as increased cortisol makes us more stress reactive and reduced testosterone makes us feel less in control. An upright and open body posture can conversely reduce our cortisol level and increase testosterone, focusing our mind and giving us the confidence to deal with challenges more proactively and skilfully.

People often pay more attention to how we communicate through our facial expression and body posture, than what we say. Studies show that when we present with an open and upright posture people are more likely to ascribe positive qualities to us and engage with us in a positive manner.

Progressive Muscle Relaxation (PMR)

Progressive muscle relaxation is a relaxation technique that has been found to be helpful for stress, anxiety, reducing pain and improving sleep. Generally speaking, a calm mind helps relax the body, and a relaxed body signals to our mind that we are safe. PMR involves tensing and then gradually releasing different muscle groups to promote physical and mental relaxation. This practice can help us become more aware of the difference between a tensed muscle and a completely relaxed muscle.

Wear some comfortable clothing. Find a place you can be free from disruptions for 10-15 minutes and get into a comfortable position whether you are sitting upright or lying down. Tune into your breath, focus on finding a comfortable rhythm of breathing.

1. Forehead
Squeeze the muscles in your forehead, holding for 15 seconds. Feel the muscles becoming tighter and tenser. Then, slowly release the tension in your forehead while counting for 30 seconds. Notice the difference in how your muscles feel as you relax. Continue to release the tension until your forehead feels completely relaxed. Breathe slowly and evenly.

2. Jaw
Tense the muscles in your jaw, holding for 15 seconds. Then release the tension slowly while counting for 30 seconds. Notice the feeling of relaxation and continue to breathe slowly and evenly.

3. Neck and Shoulders
Increase tension in your neck and shoulders by raising your shoulders up toward your ears and hold for 15 seconds.

Slowly release the tension as you count for 30 seconds. Notice the tension melting away.

4. Arms and Hands
Slowly draw both hands into fists. Pull your fists into your chest and hold for 15 seconds, squeezing as tight as you can. Then slowly release while you count for 30 seconds. Notice the feeling of relaxation.

5. Buttocks
Slowly increase tension in your buttocks over 15 seconds. Then, slowly release the tension over 30 seconds. Notice the tension melting away. Continue to breathe slowly and evenly.

6. Legs
Slowly increase the tension in your quadriceps and calves over 15 seconds. Squeeze the muscles as hard as you can. Then gently release the tension over 30 seconds. Notice the tension melting away and the feeling of relaxation that is left.

7. Feet
Slowly increase the tension in your feet and toes. Tighten the muscles as much as you can. Then slowly release the tension while you count for 30 seconds. Notice all the tension melting away. Continue breathing slowly and evenly.

Enjoy the feeling of relaxation sweeping through your body. Continue to breathe slowly and evenly.

The Power of Nature

It has been known and accepted for a very long time that nature is good for our health and wellbeing and can inspire us with awe and wonder or induce a deep sense of peace and belonging. This idea is found across cultures and has been written about over the centuries by many poets, writers, physicians, teachers, composers and politicians. Why is this? In recent years the scientific evidence for how this happens is mounting up.

In short it is now clear that being in and engaging with the natural world activates our parasympathetic nervous system (our relaxation response), reduces sympathetic nervous system activity (our stress response), improves immune function and has a generally positive impact on our physical and mental health. There are countless studies showing that people who have even the most cursory contact with the natural world have better health outcomes than those who don't. For example, here are a few of the specific findings:

Phytonicides
These volatile antimicrobial organic compounds released by plants and trees reduce blood pressure, boost immune system functioning and alter autonomic nervous system activity. As well as this they change serotonin profiles and reduce the stress response.

Mycobacterium vaccae
Found in soil these organisms show a link to improved immune functioning.

Negative air ions
Found in high concentrations in forests or mountainous areas and near moving water, these particles have shown a link to reducing depression.

Natural sights, sounds and smells
Seeing, hearing and smelling the natural world reduces sympathetic nervous system activity (our stress response) and increases parasympathetic activity (our relaxation response) and has also been linked to lowering blood pressure and enhancing immune response.

So we can see that there is plenty of research evidence pointing to how the natural world has an overall beneficial impact on our mental and physical wellbeing.

In one study, children with an ADHD diagnosis were found to concentrate significantly better after a 20 minute walk in nature as compared to a walk in an urban environment. After the nature walk children with an ADHD diagnosis scored as well on tests for concentration as children without ADHD, leading to the conclusion that the walk in nature seemed to erase their ADHD symptoms.

If you would like to find out more about the science behind the benefits of the natural world then a great place to start is the website of an innovative charity called 'Dose of Nature' (https://www.doseofnature.org.uk).

Try this:

Go for a for a walk in any green space you can get access to. Find a place to sit down and take in the sights, sounds and smells of your environment. Really focus your attention on the natural world around you. You could even try some slow breathing. Afterwards notice how you feel.

Thought Suppression

We have a natural tendency to turn away from and suppress unpleasant thoughts and feelings. Intuitively, that response makes sense, in that we seemingly protect ourselves from discomfort. However, what we know is that the energy we put into pushing something away from us often backfires. The following exercise illustrates this point:

Close your eyes for about a minute. During that time, try your best not to think about the word 'pink elephant'. When the minute is up think about what happened to the pink elephant, did you think about it or not?

This experience is based on a study in Cognitive Psychology where participants were asked to read a list of words and phrases, one of which was 'pink elephant'. Both groups were told to read the list of words, but one group was instructed not to think about the phrase 'pink elephant'. The participants who were told not to think about pink elephants, reported thinking about this much more than the other participants. Several studies since have demonstrated that suppressing thoughts tend to have the opposite effect. Whilst we will find it very difficult not to think about 'pink elephants' or other unwanted images, what we can do is shift our focus of attention. In the next section we'll look at this in more detail.

Attention

We can think of attention like a spotlight; whatever is under the spotlight gets illuminated and magnified. It appears that we have evolved a negativity bias when it comes to our attention and memory.

The neuroscientist Nick Hanson described this very aptly;

'the brain is like teflon for positive information and velcro for negative information'

It can seem unfair and unhelpful that negative information can dominate our mind to such an extent. However, this is linked with survival; our mind will prioritise information about risks and mistakes, as ignoring this could pose a threat to our survival. Although our attention might immediately focus on a threat or a mistake, we have some choice in how we redirect our attention (when safe to do so) onto things that are more helpful/constructive. Next time you find yourself focussing on a difficult event or topic, see if you can change the focus of your attention to a soothing memory, event or place.

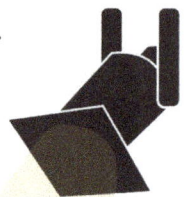

26

Power of Imagery

Our brain has an incredible capacity to create images of our external world. In fact these images can be so powerful that simply imagining an event, can be almost as impactful as experiencing it in the present moment.

Some people who have lived through traumatic events may experience distressing memories in the form of flashbacks or nightmares. Simply remembering these events, activates the limbic system in our brain, activating the fight, flight and freeze response and flushing our body with stress hormones. It feels like re-experiencing rather than simply remembering the trauma.

Equally distressing can be imagining a future event going horribly wrong, which in a similar way will activate the fight, flight and freeze mode, leaving us in a heightened state of distress.

We can harness the power of imagination and generate or activate positive images and memories that can give rise to feelings of safeness, confidence and hope.

If we bring to mind an image of our favourite meal, we may start salivating as we 'trick' the brain into believing we are about to consume food. In a similar way, we can activate our neuro circuitry to release hormones that can have a calming effect on us.

Safe Place Imagery

The aim of this practice is to create a place in your mind that you can escape to when things are difficult. The first step is to create this place, so use your imagination freely in creating your ideal safe place.

Find somewhere you can sit comfortably, without too much noise or disruption. Get into a comfortable position (upright, open and relaxed), close your eyes and settle into a relaxing rhythm of breathing.

Think of a place where you feel safe and comfortable.

It could be anywhere you like, the beach, woodlands, in the mountains or in a house or cabin. Take a good look around you in that place, notice the colours and shapes, what else can you see?

Now notice the sounds around you, or perhaps the silence. Sounds far away and nearer to you. Those that are more noticeable and those that are more subtle.

Then think about the smells you notice there. Next focus on your skin sensations, the ground underneath you, temperature, the movement of air.

Pay attention to the pleasant physical sensations in your body whilst you enjoy your safe place.

Download a recording of a guided safe place imagery practice at the following website: www.reallifepsychology.org/train-your-brain

Self Compassion

Life can be very challenging and at times feel a bit like an obstacle course. Everyone's journey through life is unique and the relative fortune and misfortune is certainly not evenly shared out. However, we will all face losses and disappointments, and despite our best efforts and intentions, we will make mistakes and bad decisions.

How we respond to these difficulties makes a big difference to how much we suffer.

The Buddhist parable of the second arrow can help us make sense of suffering and how to manage it.

In this parable it is said that when we suffer misfortune two arrows can strike us. The first of them is the misfortune itself, but the second 'arrow' is our reaction to what has happened, the thoughts and feelings that go on within us. Interestingly, within Buddhist philosophy, the second arrow is often described as the more dangerous one.

So, if I fall over and really hurt myself, do I blame myself, calling myself an idiot? Or, do I metaphorically give myself a hand up, acknowledge the pain I'm feeling and try to soothe and comfort myself?

A common observation is that we tend to be more understanding, forgiving and helpful in response to other people's suffering than our own.

Many people have had the unpleasant experience of being shouted at for making a mistake by an impatient/critical teacher or instructor. Although it's important to recognise and work towards reducing mistakes, these verbal attacks rarely help us learn. Research also shows that when we launch a verbal self-attack (such as calling ourself an idiot for making a mistake), it can result in a limbic highjack, shutting down the Cortex, the part of our brain that helps us take in and process new information. With limited access to the Cortex, we are making the process of learning much harder and we are more likely to make mistakes.

Self-compassion is not about evading responsibility or 'letting ourselves off the hook', but developing a kinder, more supportive relationship with ourselves to help us deal with challenges we face in a skilful way. Sometimes a self-compassionate act requires real courage and discipline, such as giving up reliance on drugs or alcohol to deal with difficult emotions.

Notice your internal monologue. When you are going through a difficult time, maybe after you've made a mistake or a bad decision, make a note of what you are saying to yourself.
Is it fair/unfair? Helpful/unhelpful? Kind/unkind? Enabling/disabling?

29

The Compassionate Companion

This is another imagery practice that can be very helpful, particularly if you are going through a particularly tough time or struggling with self-blame and self-criticism.

The idea here is to create an imaginary person who has the compassionate qualities you value. Try not to pick a real person as all humans are fallible, but you can use various compassionate qualities from people you know or have heard about.

Once you have created your compassionate companion and written down their traits or attributes, imagine being in the company of the compassionate companion, paying attention to what it feels like in your mind and body to have someone giving you their full attention. Someone who deeply cares about your wellbeing.

Try filling out the form below to create a compassionate companion.

How would you like your ideal caring, compassionate companion to look/appear – visual qualities?

_____
_____
_____
_____

How would you like your ideal caring, compassionate companion to sound, e.g. tone of voice?

_____
_____
_____
_____

What other sensory qualities can you give to it?

_____
_____
_____
_____

How would you like your ideal caring, compassionate companion to relate to you?

_____
_____
_____
_____

How would like to relate to your ideal caring, compassionate companion?

_____
_____
_____
_____

Avoidance

In the same way as we tend to push away and distract from negative thoughts and feelings, we can also get into a pattern of avoiding situations that give rise to this discomfort. The more anxious we feel, the stronger the urge to avoid what is making us anxious. At the time, it may seem like the only possible option. However, by continuously avoiding situations we fear, we tend to confirm our belief that the challenges we face are insurmountable and that we haven't got what it takes to deal with these situations successfully. We may experience that our world shrinks and there are fewer and fewer things we feel confident or comfortable doing. At this point, life can seem pretty gloomy and we may struggle to find a reason to get up in the morning.

The urge to retreat when we are feeling anxious is certainly not unique to humans. Rangers and farmers observed that Bison and domestic cattle that grazed on the vast Rocky Mountain plains in the US had a very different way of responding to a regular storm phenomenon in the area. As the storm travelled from West to East, the Bison charged into the storm, thereby spending less time in the eye of the storm. In contrast, the domestic cattle, huddled together and anxiously moved away from the storm, but consequently were caught up in the storm for longer periods and were more affected by it.

We can all benefit from taking a lesson from the Bison in facing our fears head on. We might experience that our negative assumptions don't materialise and that we cope that little bit better than we had predicted.

Try this:

Write a list of things you would like to do, but avoid doing out of fear of not being able to manage.

List these activities in order of difficulty, starting with the least difficult first.

For example, you may be struggling with social anxiety and you would like to build up your confidence to one day being able to go to a gig with friends. Step 1 might be to go to the local shop on your own when it's quiet, Step 2 might be to visit the same place at a busier time. Step 3 may be a visit to a café on your own at a quiet time and Step 4 might be to go when it's busier.

See if you can identify what's your number 10 and number 1 and populate the steps in-between. If you break your goals into manageable chunks, you might find that as you are progressing through the steps, you anxiety lessens, your confidence grows and step 10 might feel within reach. Remember even the smallest steps are progress and will help you to feel less anxious over time.

Belief Systems

As young beings we try to make sense of the world around us. This process of making meaning gives rise to what we call core beliefs; deeply held ideas about ourselves, others and the world.

We use our beliefs to understand and navigate this world, through rules and strategies for living.

For example, if we have developed a belief that crossing a road can be dangerous, we automatically look right and left and ensure the road is clear before we make a swift crossing.

We are particularly impressionable early in life and the words and actions of people in authority, eg., parents, teachers, a close friend, the popular boy or girl in school, shape our core beliefs in important ways. Core beliefs are strongly held and once formed they can be hard to change as they are typically maintained by our tendency to focus on information that supports the core belief and ignore evidence that contradicts it.

If a parent keeps telling us we are stupid when we were young, this may translate into a strong core belief that persists into adulthood, despite plenty of evidence that we actually are rather capable.

We may acknowledge the evidence that we are capable, yet we don't feel capable because of our fixed core belief.

Often core beliefs develop over time, but they can also change as a result of an isolated incident. For example, we may conclude from our early life that we are safe and in control and live in a safe world. However, if one day we are the victim on a random, unprovoked attack, immediately, we feel vulnerable and see the world as unsafe and something we need to hide from.

If a young child experiences physical abuse growing up, they may reasonably develop a belief that they are vulnerable, that others can't be trusted and the world is unsafe. In fact, whilst these things are happening these beliefs are true, which is why they are formed.

Such experiences and the beliefs they cause can give rise to necessary, protective strategies, such as hypervigilance (always looking for danger) and keeping people at arm's length.

However, once this young child grows up into an adult who can now defend themselves, and may live in a safe environment, these beliefs and strategies may no longer be protective, but act as a barrier to living life fully. In this way, the self-protective beliefs we developed in childhood become self-limiting beliefs in adulthood.

The three Ps of Pessimism – Personalisation, Permanence and Pervasiveness – can play an important role in how we are affected by the difficulties we experience.

Personalisation is thinking that the problem is only due to our own fault or defect, instead of considering other factors that may have played a role in the problem occurring.

Permanence is thinking that a bad situation will last forever, that bad things will always happen and good things never happen.

Pervasiveness is thinking a mistake or bad situation applies across all areas of your life. For example, "I failed this exam, I fail at everything I do".

Common negative core beliefs about ourselves include being unsafe/vulnerable, not being in control, being incapable, not feeling worthy and being unlikeable/unloveable. People often develop beliefs that others are judgmental, unkind, uncaring, untrustworthy and we may see the world as unsafe, unpredictable or unfair. We may also develop belief systems about negative thoughts and feelings, which lead us to feel unable to control them.

We tend to act as if our core beliefs are factual and we rarely question the truthfulness and usefulness of these beliefs. However, doing a thorough review of our core beliefs can be helpful as we may be guided by out of date, untrue and limiting core beliefs that give rise to negative thoughts and feelings and unhelpful behaviours that stop us living life fully.

Write a list of beliefs you have developed about:

- Yourself
- The World
- People around you
- Negative thoughts and feelings

Then think about whether these beliefs are accurate, reflective of your current self and situation, enabling or limiting.

33

Perspective Taking

Imagine you are walking through town and a good friend walks straight past you, without acknowledging you. What is going through your mind? How do you feel (emotionally and bodily)?

What do you think you might do next? Think about how you might think, feel and act if you made the following conclusion from this situation:

1) They didn't see me
2) They saw me and simply didn't feel like saying 'hi'
3) They were going through a particularly tough time and couldn't face talking to anyone

Often, we make an assumption about a situation or person, e.g. 'he doesn't like me', 'I'm going to mess this up'. If these assumptions are left unchallenged, they often convert into 'facts'.

However, noticing that certain negative thoughts and assumption cause us distress, can remind us to take a step back and questions these thoughts.

Is what I'm thinking/saying to myself true (any real evidence for this)?
Is it helpful (will it help me deal with the situation more skillfully)?
Is it kind (would I say this to someone I care about)?

Have a look at the list of thinking styles on the next page and see which applies to you. Are there particular situations where these thought patterns are more common for you?

How do these thoughts make you feel? And act?

All or nothing thinking.
Sometimes called 'black and white thinking'
"If I'm not perfect I have failed" "Either I do it right or not at all"

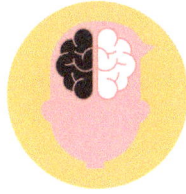

Blowing things out of proportion
(catastrophising), or inappropriately shrinking something to make it seem less important

Only paying attention to certain types of evidence
Noticing our failures but not seeing our successes

I feel embarrassed so I must be an idiot
Assuming that because we feel a certain way what we think must be true

There are two key types of jumping to conclusion
Mind reading: imagining we know what others are thinking
Fortune telling: predicting the future

Over generalising
"Everything is always rubbish" "Nothing good ever happens"
Seeing a pattern based upon a single event, or being overly broad in the conclusions we draw

Disqualifying the positive
Discounting the good things that have happened or that you have done for some reason or another:
That doesn't count

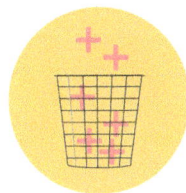

Using critical words like 'should', 'must', or 'ought'
can make us feel guilty, or like we have already failed. If we apply 'shoulds' to other people the result is often frustration

Assigning labels to ourselves or other people.
"I'm a loser"
"I'm completely useless"
"They're such an idiot"

Personalisation
Blaming yourself or taking responsibility for something that wasn't completely your fault. Conversely, blaming other people for something that was your fault

Thought Balancing

This is a commonly used exercise to help re-evaluate how we are looking at things. Try using it if you find yourself feeling low or anxious about something that has happened in your day.

	Example
Trigger (what situation gave rise to what I'm feeling/ thinking right now)	I failed my math's exam
Unhelpful/ distressing thought	I'm stupid, I always mess things up I'll be kicked out of college I'll never get a job
Feeling (emotionally and bodily)	Upset Anxious Angry Deflated Tense
Helpful/ kind thought	It's not true I always mess things up I've been doing OK in college this year Maths isn't my strongest subject and I was ill the week leading up to the exam so couldn't revise as much as I had planned This result is unlikely to have a bearing on my overall grades in college or job prospects
Feeling (emotionally and bodily)	A bit frustrated but not angry and feeling a bit more hopeful I can bounce back from this Less tense

Now you have a go!

Trigger (what situation gave rise to what I'm feeling/ thinking right now)	

Unhelpful/ distressing thought	

Feeling (emotionally and bodily)	

Helpful/ kind thought	

Feeling (emotionally and bodily)	

Building Resilience

You may have had repeated experiences of failure in life, that can contribute to low confidence and self-efficacy (perceived control over our behaviour and social environment).

This in turn may lead you to avoiding challenges and opportunities for learning and growing, as you may expect, or fear, another failure.

In order to build our confidence, motivation and commitment to learning, it's important to develop positive beliefs about mastery and control. It may be that you struggle to give up substances, stay in a relationship, attend health appointments etc., but chances are there are some things you do well and consistently, despite many obstacles.

We can also have a tendency to pay more attention to the things we can't do rather than what we can do. Imagine someone takes their dog out for a walk twice a day, come rain and shine. They may not necessarily see this as an act of resilience, but in order to persist with this activity, they need to overcome various challenges.

We may be faced with cold, icy or wet weather on occasions, maybe aches or pains some days, or social anxiety and low mood. It can be helpful to identify the strategies that help us overcome these barriers.

Perhaps I've got myself some warm, rain-proof clothes that I have ready when the weather is bad. I may remind myself that a warm shower and some stretches help ease my aches, and focusing on calming my breathing and bringing to mind the smiley dogwalker I always see on my walk helped me feel a little more relaxed.

I may also remind myself that the initial anxiety I feel setting off on my walk is soon replaced with a sense of achievement and joy seeing the wagging tail of my dog! We can develop our resilience by applying the strategies we know work for the things we do consistently and apply them to an area our lives where we struggle to stay committed.

List the obstacles you face when carrying out your chosen activity.

Apply your new resilient strategies and see if this helps you improve your commitment in this area.

Gratitude

As we have seen, we are very good at focusing on and remembering negatives, and sometimes an isolated mistake can ruin an entire day or week. This can affect our mood and motivation and contribute to shaping a pessimistic view of ourself and our surroundings.

A gratitude practice is a good way to help appreciate and remember positive experiences, however fleeting or trivial they way seem.

Sometimes there may be obvious positives in our day, other times it may feel like looking for a needle in a haystack. There are no hard and fast rules to doing a gratitude practice. The idea is simply to spend a little bit of time, perhaps towards the end of the day, to reflect on positives. It may be a positive comment or feedback from a friend, appreciate the warmth of the sun on an otherwise cold, bleak day. Something funny or enlightening you read or heard about. Sometimes, this includes reframing a difficult experience: rather than focusing on a mistake, shift the focus to what you learnt from a mistake. Perhaps you responded to this in a creative, skilful manner.

Try this:

Think about a recent day that was difficult for you. First, focus on a negative or difficult aspect of the day and pay attention to how it affects your mood and body. Second, try to focus on anything positive that day and linger on those experiences. Do you notice a shift in how your mood and body feels?

Online Relationships

Nowadays we can easily spend an ever increasing amount of time on various social media platforms.

Clearly there are numerous advantages to being able to connect in this way. However, the evidence around social media as a way to connect with others is mixed. Overall, evidence indicates that spending extended periods of time on social media might be bad for our mental health.

It appears that the hormones that facilitate good mood (serotonin), motivation (dopamine) and trust and bonding (oxytocin) aren't released in the same way when we meet through a screen. Further to this, one clear risk identified is from platforms with more of a focus on imagery, such as Instagram and Pinterest, where filters and perceived perfection are the 'norm'.

When we are in a bad place, we are more likely to make unfair and unfavorable comparisons with others, comparing our inside experience to the representations of people's lives posted online. We zoom in on and magnify our perceived inadequacies and compare this to the digitally enhanced photos and inflated profiles on social media, leaving us feeling inadequate and low.

Clearly, social media is here to stay and it brings with it lots of benefits, so the solution may not be to get rid of it altogether. Rather, we perhaps need to ensure that we have time and energy to cultivate relationships face to face and not rely entirely on the virtual world.

Relationships

Relationships are key to wellbeing, and they can be the biggest source of comfort or trauma. Interpersonal trauma tends to cause more severe and longer lasting distress than accidents and natural disasters. If we are lucky to have people we can rely on in times of adversity, not only do we recover from psychological trauma quicker, but also our physical recovery is speeded up.

As mammals
we are hardwired
to connect
with our caregivers.

This quote from evolutionary psychology illustrates:

'Bees have evolved to live in a hive and humans have evolved to live in a tribe.'

We learn to relate to others by observing how people in our tribe relate to each other and how our primary caregivers relate to us.

These relational experiences translate into an inner working model of relationships we call attachment styles. If our caregivers offer protection, comfort and age appropriate autonomy, we are likely to develop what we call a 'secure attachment style'.

Adults with secure attachment styles tend to feel safe and comfortable sharing feelings with others and are able to lean on others in difficult times, but they also have a high degree of self-contentment and self-reliance.

If our caregivers on the other hand don't offer sufficient protection or comfort, and are dismissive, critical or violent in response to us reaching out for support, we are likely to develop either an insecure-anxious attachment style or an insecure-avoidant attachment style.

Someone who is anxiously attached, will often cling on to their partner, fearing that they will leave them. This may result in feeling suffocated and then withdrawal, confirming the belief that people don't stay.

A person with an insecure-avoidant attachment style, will often keep others at arms length, and insist on doing everything themselves, resulting in more fleeting and supeficial relationships, leaving the person feeling alone and uncared for.

If we have developed either an insecure-anxious or insecure-avoidant attachment style, it doesn't mean we can't develop good, intimate relationships. If we are aware of our attachment style and the challenges this might bring in developing a close connection, we can learn different ways of communicating and relating to others, and as such our attachment style might change over time.

Whether we see ourselves as a natural introvert or extrovert, we all need relationships in order to feel good and function well. Our relationships can then become a source of comfort and strength.

An Experiment

An experiment conducted in the US in the 1970s called 'Rat Park' illustrates the power of relationships.

In this experiment some rats were placed in a cage on their own, with access to two water supplies, one containing pure water, the other containing water laced with either cocaine or heroin.

In a second larger cage, known as 'Rat Park', many rats were placed together with lots to do and where they were free to roam, play and socialize as they wished.

In 'Rat Park' there were also two water supplies, again one with pure water and one mixed with either cocaine or heroin.

The rather remarkable finding was that the rats placed in 'Rat Park' preferred the plain water, and even when they did drink from the drug laced bottle, they did so intermittently and never overdosed. However, the rats placed in cages on their own preferred the drug laced water, often repeatedly drinking it until they overdosed and died.

In this experiment a positive social community beat the addictive pull of drugs.

Conclusions

Summary

An integral part of being human is having a brain that is busy sensing and interpreting what's going on around us, generating a near constant stream of thoughts and feelings, some pleasant, others unpleasant.

Our inner threat system is working 24/7 to identify and respond to any threats to our survival. These notifications of potential threats will cause momentary stress or anxiety, but a balanced brain is quick to identify false alarms and reassure us we are safe and well. An oversensitive threat system, maybe as a result of past traumas or stressors, struggles to discern between real and false alarm, leaving us in a heightened state of stress.

If we struggle to turn off the threat system ourselves, we may resort to substances or activities to temporarily shut the alarm off. However, this is likely to only offer temporary relief, as the stress and anxiety will resurface once we are no longer engaged in the activity.

Although we aren't able to shut off negative thoughts and feelings altogether, we can practise strategies that help balance our thoughts and calm our emotions, which in turn enable us to feel more in control and make better decisions.

Relationships are key to wellbeing.

Being able to trust, open up to and lean on others in times of difficulties can help us through adversity. The quality of our relationship with ourself is paramount to good mental health, and whether we act as a bully or friend to ourselves when the going gets tough may determine whether we sink or swim.

Evaluation

There is a saying that goes 'what we measure, we improve' and this has some backing in the psychotherapy outcome research literature. Measuring our progress or lack of it can help us reflect on what is helpful or not about our intervention, and seeing progress can motivate us to keep going and commit to self-care practices.

The scale below is a composite of various scales that are often used to measure psychological wellbeing and distress in different ways. It is not a validated scale but simply something we have put together to help you track how things are going. So we hope it can be a useful tool to track how you are doing or compare before, during and after the work on the Train Your Brain Manual.

1) Almost never   2) Not very often   3) Sometimes   4) Often   5) Almost always

		1	2	3	4	5
1.	When I'm low, I think I'm the only one who struggles like this					
2.	I really go to town on myself when I make a mistake					
3.	I try to be gentle with myself when I make a mistake or mess things up					
4.	I struggle to feel much enjoyment					
5.	I struggle with feelings of depression and hopelessness					
6.	I feel I am letting everyone down, including myself					
7.	Feeling uneasy and uncomfortable					
8.	Constant worrying					
9.	I struggle to relax					
10.	I can change the way I think about a situation and feel differently as a result					
11.	When I'm dealing with a challenging situation, I think about it in a way that makes me feel calm and in control					
12.	When I am down, I make sure I keep my negative feelings to myself					

Self Compassion: 1-3   **Depression:** 4-6

Anxiety: 7-9   **Depression:** 10-12

Reverse scores: 3, 10 and 11. To reverse score items; 1=5, 2=4, 3=3, 4=2, 5=1.

Max Score: 60. Higher scores indicate greater level of distress and greater difficulty regulating distress.

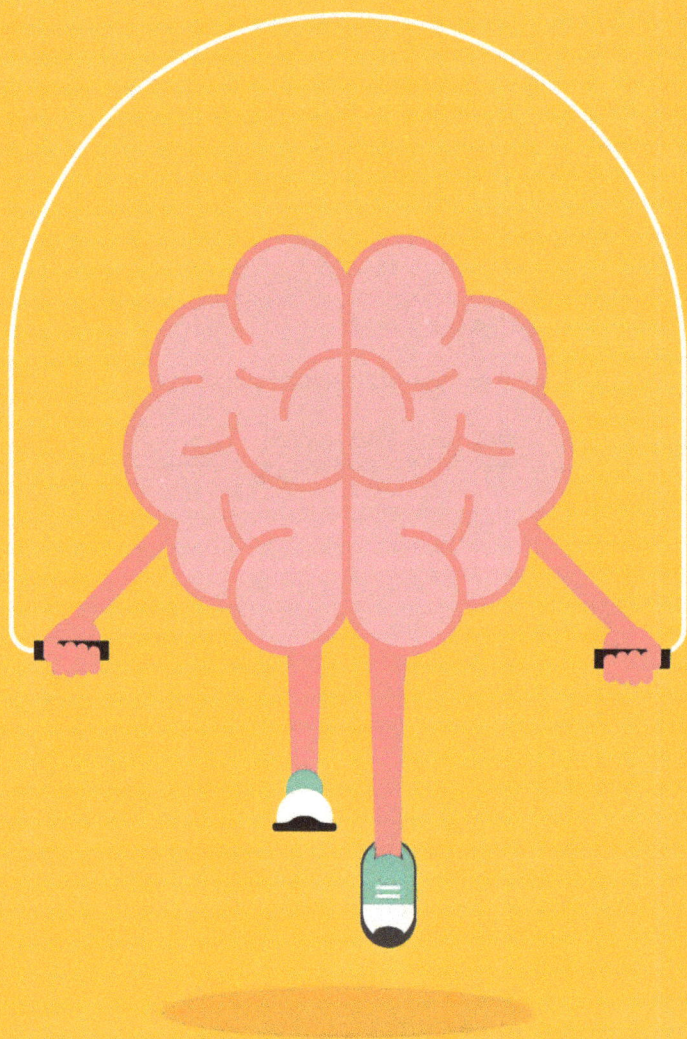

www.ingramcontent.com/pod-product-compliance
Lightning Source LLC
Chambersburg PA
CBHW061305270326
41935CB00022B/1845